ALL HEATHENS

ALL HE

ATHENS

MARIANNE CHAN

SARABANDE BOOKS
Louisville, KY

Publisher's Cataloging-In-Publication Data
(Prepared by The Donohue Group, Inc.)

Names: Chan, Marianne, author.

Title: All heathens : poems / by Marianne Chan.

Description: First edition. | Louisville, KY : Sarabande Books, [2020]

Identifiers: ISBN 9781946448521 | ISBN 9781946448538 (ebook)

Subjects: LCSH: Filipino-Americans—Poetry.

Filipino-American poetry. | LCGFT: Poetry.

Classification: LCC PS3603.H366 A45 2020 (print) | LCC PS3603.H366 (ebook)

DDC 811/.6—dc23

Cover and interior design by Alban Fischer.

Manufactured in Canada.

This book is printed on acid-free paper.

Sarabande Books is a nonprofit literary organization.

This project is supported in part by an award from the National Endowment for the Arts.
The Kentucky Arts Council, the state arts agency, supports Sarabande Books with state
tax dollars and federal funding from the National Endowment for the Arts.

For my parents, Jack and Patricia,
and my brother, Rammel

CONTENTS

I.

MOMOTARO IN THE PHILIPPINES

Here, peaches come from boxes
that smell like Europe, from cans
made of a tin-coated steel.
I lie with the peaches soaking in
saccharine darkness until freed.
I don't recognize the children
who run toward me. Their faces
like the feathers on the feet
of birds. Their slippers repeating that
melancholic drone. "Wake up," they say.
"Wake up." And as I rise from
the dreamy fluid—oh, the America,
which preserves me—I press
my sticky forehead on your sun-
freckled hand. I love you, am sorry,
am not a warrior, no hero. I
fight for nothing, am stingy. I ate
all the peaches from the can
from the box from which I came.

LANSING SINULOG REHEARSAL, 2010

January in Michigan means Viva Pit Senyor, aluminum trays
heavy with pancit, dinuguan, pinakbet, caldereta, lumpia,

leche flan, bibingka, and five Hot-N-Ready pizzas for
the husbands and children. My mother is wearing paint

on her face, a candle on her head. You see, Sinulog is not
just a religious holiday, but a festival, a performance.

If no one will remember our history, then we will reenact
a version every year, even if a January blizzard is coming

through, Michigan-style, in which the trees die standing,
and the roads are as treacherous as the early modern

seas. Still, we sashay into the community center, wrapped
in polyester fibers and fake leather gloves. We slide off

our sodden boots, go barefooted. In this performance
of our history, someone's white husband plays Magellan.

This husband used to work for GM before the auto-
industry crisis. Now he is unemployed and enjoying his

role as a powerful yet bumbling navigator, captain-general.
The actor's wife is playing a native Filipina. She has no lines,

only dances, but in reality, she talks fast and uncensored
like a late-night radio DJ. Because I'm a teenager, she teaches

me the Bisaya word for masturbation, and throughout
the rehearsal, I can't stop saying it: lulo. My dad tells me

to stop, for goodness' sake, but why should I, when everyone
is laughing, and the word is perfect. Lulo, I say. Lulo.

All the Filipina wives are playing native dancers, and their
husbands are playing conquistadors, because what were

conquistadors if not small-town men with beer breath
wearing plastic armor, holding a figurine of a brown baby

Jesus while a native woman throws them the keys to their
Buick sedan asking them to grab the paper plates. We'll need

paper plates, since this rehearsal involves eating as much food
as we'll eat at the real party so we'll know if our costumes

still fit. Most of these husbands met their wives on the internet,
but in the 1500s, it was a little different. You got on a boat

first to find spices or gold or coconuts or unconditional
love. Someone's muscular Fil Am son plays Lapu-Lapu,

who in real-life Filipino history, is known for slaying Magellan
with an iron sword before Magellan could make his way

around the world. Magellan was probably killed by a group
of native folks—not just one Filipino guy—but we like this

version of the story because it is a historical representation
of the conflictedness we feel on the inside. And who doesn't

love a good one-on-one fight? If Manny Pacquiao lived in Lansing,
he could've been our Lapu-Lapu, and our Magellan (Ron)

wouldn't have stood a chance, the poor guy. An obstetrician
from Baguio plays a smart Enrique of Malacca, Magellan's slave

and translator (who may have betrayed Magellan's crew after his
death, but we're not mentioning that here), and an accountant

from Manila plays Raja Humabon, the king who converted
to Catholicism as an act of diplomacy. I am Princess Amihan,

the king's wife. I am also the director of this wacky, factually
dubious play, and I tell Magellan that he should stop doing

that thing with his shoulders, and I tell Lapu-Lapu to learn his
godforsaken lines, and I yell at the dancers to stop chattering,

because this is serious, because the performance is tomorrow,
and we've got to do this right. And my mother keeps telling me

that I should move my hips when I dance, because I am as stiff
as a Methodist church in the suburbs, and I weep because I

will never dance as beautifully as she does, and I will never
be who she wants me to be: a nurse. No way can I make it

through nursing school, when I am the director of this play.
And tomorrow, everyone will scrape the ice off their windows,

and carry the food in the trunks of their American cars. They
will say their lines. I will say my lines, and I won't say lulo, though I

will be tempted to say it, before the lights go down, and the drums
start beating hard like a heart from the boombox speakers,

and before the community center fills with brown faces, laughing
and cheering, because this play is for all of us, it is our reckoning.

ELEGY FOR YOUR MASTER

for Enrique of Malacca, Magellan's slave

There wasn't enough rain
to kill him. The ship stayed
afloat, your clothing
darkened, practically dry

beneath the stormed sun.
What Master wants: tuyok.
Circumnavigation—to travel
all the way around—

until you are back
to where you started,
until we feast on what is
East. Until West swallows

West. He bought your body
with a few coins from his pocket.
He will return it when he is
dead, when you are twenty-six,

your heart, a brown
spinning globe. He will
turn and return you,
tuyok—back to your body.

In *circumnavigation*,
the past is in front of you,
waiting to be refound,
rediscovered, but you will

arrive, and the people
have aged. And now, you
pray for his soul. Because
he has made you Christian.

WHEN THE MAN AT THE PARTY SAID HE
WANTED TO OWN A FILIPINO

I should've said that all I've ever wanted was to own
a fifty-year-old white man (which is what he was),
but I didn't say that, because it wasn't true. Instead, I said

nothing, but I almost said, amicably: Yes, our bodies
are banging, aren't they? Our skin is leather upholstery
beneath the savage sun, our eyes are fruits fallen

from the highest trees, the bottoms of our unshod feet
the color of amethyst. I almost said: We will parade
around your living room in a linen cloth and feed you

turtle eggs and cornioles meat from a porcelain dish.
I almost said: I'll be your Filipino, you be my Viking.
We'll ride in a boat together. I'll wear your horny

helmet. But I said nothing. At that party, I wanted
to be liked, which is my tragic flaw. I always find myself
on the street smiling at people who look to be neo-Nazis.

I call it a safety smile. Rarely do they smile back,
but I would hug them if they needed it, if I think it
would spare me. I used to wonder if this amenability

was inherited. Raja Humabon, a Filipino king
in the 1500s, did not resist Magellan's missionary agenda.
Humabon greeted Magellan and his Christian lord

with friendship. Maybe out of genuine religious feeling,
or maybe servitude and friendship are a type of fire
retardant, protection from the torches that burned down

the villages of the chiefs who refused to kneel. Of course,
there were some who refused to kneel, and maybe this is
also something inherited, along with everything else,

all the possible variations, and it doesn't take me long to
realize the flaws in this notion of an inherited friendliness.
When I was thirteen or fourteen, the white husband

of my parents' friend showed me pictures of his Filipino
wife in different bikinis, the ones she sent him
in letters before he hopped on a plane to the Philippines

to marry her. He had a five-by-seven album full of these photographs,
these flirtations. It made him nostalgic to sift through them.
"What's good about my wife," he said, "is that she's easy

on the eyes." A tuft of his chest hair appeared from the collar
in his shirt, and the soul inside of me nearly choked on its
own regurgitations. Before I could ask if he'd sent her

pictures of himself, I heard his wife's bright cackle from
the other room, like the firing of artillery from a distant ship.
I noted that she was not easy on the ears, that she was

not easy at all. I realize now that this story was never about us
being owned, because we will always own ourselves. This story
is about the way the world believes that it owns us, holding

its album of pictures in its wishful hands. And we are not
amenable as much as we are insidious. We are the cornioles,
who, after being eaten alive by a whale, enter the whale's body

and take small, tender bites of the whale's enormous heart.

A COUNTRY OF BEAUTIFUL WOMEN

There are millions of short people
in this Snow White. Short only

by comparison, which is how
the short people lived their lives:

relative to. S's skin is lighter than Y's
is lighter than C's is lighter

than Q's. Lightness, as if the dark
were synonymous with heavy.

Darkness: the dead weight
of her mother and father combined.

Take a moment to admire her
colonial derma, the white

pigment of a Spanish church.
Take a picture, it will last longer

amidst the gunfire. In this story,
mirrors reflect other people's

furniture. Beauty is in the eye
of the purveyors of shabu

at the market. Watch as our girl
lifts her skirt to hear them howl.

And she wonders—as she presses
her dewy forehead to her stepmother's

sun-spotted hand, as she kneels
before her figurine of the Virgin,

a white woman in a satin robe,
if a prince—any prince—will

dislodge the apple from her throat.
She asks her ginuo for a sign. He

tells her: "though your sins are scarlet,
they shall be white as snow." Whiteness,

the night is heavy. Lightness:
the hands of a country lifting her up.

ORIGIN STORY

1.

Not Eve, but Eve's Filipino half sister, bad dancer, lute player, naked and fat, fermenting grains, painting veins with berries and clay, shoots the shit with snake and tree beneath moonlight, while God, Eve, and even Adam make fires in caves, drawing pictures of buffalo and horses on walls, like a bunch of wacko, hallucinating tunnel dwellers.

2.

"When you were born," my mother tells me, "you resembled our statue of Buddha." Not the thin icon, not the skeletal, ascetic Siddhārtha Gautama, but Pu-Tai, the fat one in American Chinese restaurants, symbol of abundance and generosity. She says: "You always drank too much soda. Your father gave you whatever you wanted, even if it wasn't good for you. That is why you were happy." Hedonism is not natured, but nurtured. As she finishes telling me this, she stretches her stout body along the loveseat in her newly bought suit. She burps after her snack of fried chicken. She asks me to rub her feet while she watches *Jeopardy!*, and then, she offers to rub mine.

3.

Not Eve, but Eve's serpent, imbibing fruit juices and writhing her leggy body on the branch of a tree. I always imagined that the serpent had the legs of a seductive woman in black nylons before God took them away as punishment. Maybe she wanted them to go. She wanted to feel the earth, her origin, warm on her belly. Where are the legs now? Perhaps, at the bottom of the ocean, alongside the remains of the ark, a pair of ancient nylons is steadily disintegrating.

4.

"When you were born," my father tells me, "you looked just like I did." He hands me a black-and-white picture of himself in a crib, a weeping baby. How pleasurable it is, as a child, to instantly find your origins in some earlier being. The future is predestined. I see my eyes in his eyes, his crooked gait in my crooked gait. I look up at my father. I think: In a few years, I will be a sixty-year-old Chinese man with a black-and-white mustache.

5.

Not Eve, but eve. Before my father was my father's father, a man who had twenty children with numerous women, a man who drank and smoked and did not wish to die. Before my mother was my mother's mother, a woman who lost her legs, like the wonderful, wise serpent who initiated life and earthly joys. Eve. The day that comes before an important day. A name given after shame. My brother tells me that when I was born I had a mark on my head that resembled a tree, and it grew fruit until it disappeared. That's a myth. The truth of the story: after us, there will be another, then another, then another.

MY MOTHER TELLS ME ABOUT LOLO

It was a Friday, the temperature tepid,
a perfect day for a trim, my hair down
to my waist. Your lolo—with his
penchant for tinkering, his amateurish
hair-salon posture—snipped eight inches
off my head easily like tags on newly
bought merchandise. Such cavalierness,
such lack of precision. I saw my new
hairdo and cried hard for my lost locks,
my diminished strength. I, a little-girl
Samson. He, my Delilah. I wept for
hours, until he patted me on the shoulders,
said—"It's okay, inday, it will grow!
It will grow!" When my hair came back,
he never again approached me with a pair
of scissors. He reserved his hair-related
experiments for his sons, who also
found themselves weeping in front
of mirrors after he left them as patchy
and lopsided as the stray dogs who
chased the Jeeps in Carbon. Again, he
replied, "Mga amaw! Don't cry! It will
grow back!" And years later, when I lived
in Germany, when your dad was
deployed, I brought you home
to the Philippines. You got sick,

had a fever, lost weight so fast no one
knew what to do. My father spit on your
neck, told you, "Inday, you will grow,"
and soon, you were healthy again, as if this
was some incantation, some heathen
magic he knew. He died shortly after that,
still young and handsome as César
Ramírez. They gelled his hair, sprinkled
a little cologne behind his ears. They
torched his body, he shrank into ashes.
Years later, when they amputated my
mother's gangrened legs, he wasn't
around to say: "Don't worry. They will grow
back." And when Death took my mother,
my brothers, he wasn't alive to tell the ones
left behind: "They will grow, they will
all grow, they will all grow back." And he
was right to be dead and silent. No one
who has died has ever returned, has ever
grown back from the loam. We prayed
for resurrections, but the dead remain
as memories that seem to shrink
in the mind, like an airplane appearing
smaller the further it gets from the ground.

JET LAG

Dream that you are asleep
beneath a mosquito net
next to your mother
who is always singing.
Forget that you are sixty.
Time flies when you're
surviving with rice to eat,
people to talk to, insulin
injections to your belly.
Wake up with *Mama*
on the back of your throat
like the bone of a fish, caught.
Forget that she is long gone.
It's been almost twenty years.
Longer since she lost her legs.
Remember? Memory travels
through several time zones,
rises up in the air for hours. It is
the checked bag you thought
would never arrive, but was,
all along, waiting for you
on the carousel, one you didn't
recognize. Decide which bag
to carry on. Decide what

becomes anniversaries,
what to long for, what lyrics
to sing, when to keep
sleeping, when to wake up.

ON BUZZ ALDRIN'S BIRTHDAY

Now I see the Moon in a far different light—not as a destination but more a point of departure.

        —BUZZ ALDRIN

1.

In the moon's thin atmosphere,
a footprint or movement
of dust may stay in the same place
for centuries. In 1969,

when Buzz Aldrin considered
the moon a destination,
he left his footprint, and it clings
to her face like a scar. On earth,

the body changes. Gravity
yanks, the sun sheds its skin,
people age. People, our bodies:
always at a point of departure.

But the mind
has its sundry destinations
where it lands to find
sources of water.

2.

In 1997, I fly with my mother
to the Philippines to attend
my grandmother's funeral.
To my parents, America

was never a destination,
simply a place to rest one's
feet. The Philippines was
the final stop, the inevitable

return. But on earth,
home is a fluid thing, a shape-
shifter. At my grandmother's
funeral, her home is no longer

in the body she left behind,
powdered and rouged
to resemble life. My mother
sees this and shudders. We hear

rumors of my grandfather's ghost
lingering around their village
during the hour of my grandmother's
death, to take her with him,

her point of departure.

3.

Like the moon, home changes
shape, size, and skin. Tonight,
the moon looks as thin
as a sip of wine, communion

bread. Buzz Aldrin is eighty-nine.
Perhaps he prays every day
for new planets, asteroids.
He prays retrospectively

to have been the first,
rather than the second.
When my parents fly back
to the Philippines now,

they stay for enough time
to acquire mosquito bites,
jet lag. Then, they fly back
to America where the atmosphere

is a home that keeps one praying
for peace and prosperity,
keeps one longing for other moons.

4.

In lamplight, I dream of moon-water.
In moonlight, my mother dreams
of her mother, who once dreamed
of new beaches, mangos, black sand.

My mother dreams of her father too,
who was destined to come
to America before he grew sick.
And my father dreams of his grandparents

who were destined to return to China,
but stayed on the islands,
because nations, like homes,
are a fluid thing. In starlight,

Buzz Aldrin dreams of Phobos
and Deimos: lumpy Martian moons
dangling in the night's sky. In earth-
light, moon stays awake,

insomniac, and dreams of nothing,
is merely present, as a reminder
of where we've been,
where we're destined to go.

II.

WHEN WE LIVED IN GERMANY

Walk with me now along the Rhine River, white tulips, a masked parade. We rake our leaves away from sidewalks. Take photographs of beige castles. Stay silent. Stay put. Make airplanes out of magazines. We may never fly home. We may never buy grandfather clocks from the markets. We go to Asian marts to smell the merchandise, buy shrimp paste and pay in marks instead of pesos, instead of dollars, and mark our checkbooks, mark our calendars, mark our seasons, mark our children. On our landline, long-distance, we call our grandfathers and grandmothers, voices crackling, old and island-beaten, spotted like dalmatians. Across nations, we may never see them. Through the mail, let us send our love in the form of boxes of German chocolate. Spam, Vienna sausages, canned peaches, tsenilas to line their walls. Let us nail our families to the wall in the form of pictures, in which they never move, never age, roll their cigarettes, and never die. We buy grandfather clocks we never wind. Never mind. Let us leave them. Our children are now the clocks at which we glance to measure how long, how distant, how cruel.

LOVE SONG FOR ANTONIO PIGAFETTA

The longest and most valuable narrative of the voyage was written by a young Italian who was neither a professional seaman nor humanist.

—R. A. SKELTON, *Magellan's Voyage*

I consider you a forefather, Tony, even though you were
      from Venice, and your beard held the aroma of gondolas
passing through a canal. Still, I tell people you were my great-

great-grandfather's grandfather. I always wanted to be Italian.
      When we lived in Europe, my dad would toss our sleeping
bodies in the back seat of a Honda Accord in the dead of night

to drive the six hundred kilometers to Vicenza and buy porcelain
      figurines from a man named Guillermo. We'd sell them
to the Filipino ladies in Germany who wanted to decorate

their military base apartments like palazzos. Tony, did you grow up
      in a palazzo or a basilica? When I say these words,
I don't know what they mean. I only know what I imagine

they mean. I imagine a castle made of bones, I imagine a large
      pointer bounding through a bustling market,
I imagine that you are my ancient ancestor. And you very well

may be. In your journal, you wrote that you danced

        with unshod princesses from Zzubu. My Zzubuano

mother is not from royal blood, but she is the daughter

of a woman who stuffed adobo pork in her apron pockets

        to save for later. I do always go unshod, though I don't wear

linen made from trees to cover my shameful parts. I would

if that interested you. I would wear my hair long so the ends touch

        the ground. You were a tourist, Tony, and now so are we.

In Italy, we bought seeds and fed the pigeons on the cobblestones,

and my father would say about the locals: "Their manner

        of drinking is this . . ." and "Their manner of dressing

is that. . . ." On our drive home, we exchanged porcelain

for a bowl of hot German soup, and I would sit on my feet

        and write, like you did, about our voyages. In my journal,

I wrote "ciao = hello & goodbye." This is a circular word,

used in meeting and parting, going all the way around, like the heads

        of island warriors, like the rings they wore in their ears,

like a fleet of Christian ships sailing the heathen waters.

LUNCH IS READY

for my father and Papa Jake

And the sun was hot yellow tea in a saucer, and Lola
asked the twins to go call their Lolo at the store,

and they were boys then, they ran past the bicycles,
horse carriages, pedicabs, past the ladies selling hanging

rice and tinapa, while at the tindahan, where "Summer Wind"
was always playing, and where teenage mestizo boys

with damp brown skin carried bags of salt on their heads
from trucks and into storage, the twins shouted

some of the only Cantonese words they knew: "Yak fan lo!"
they said. "Lunch is ready." And Lolo rushed home and ate

his sotanghon with black mushrooms and rice. After
the meal, the twins watched as Lolo ambled back to work,

carrying scraps of fish in a bowl for the cats. These cats
would catch the mice who fed on packages of rice, who tore

holes in his boxes of chocolates, bags of coffee, sugar,
white flour. Thank God for the cats! They were good

for business, and for that, Lolo was happy. He fed them
every day. The tindahan was a quarter mile from home,

and the twins watched from afar as the cats came to greet
Lolo, meeting him in the middle of his walk like old

friends with a message to convey. And the cats spoke
to him, told him their balita, until he reached the threshold .

of the tindahan. There, he put down the bowl of food,
and they ate. The twins watched this and said nothing,

only looked at each other. They didn't need words
to communicate the feeling—Lolo, the cats, it was a kind

of magic. The twins were not afraid of him. He gave them
their nickname. "Pahak," he said, and it was wonderful,

so wonderful to have a nickname, to be called something,
anything that was not the names their parents gave

them. Pahak, in Bisaya, means scar on the back of the head.
And when they heard the ducks beneath the floorboards

saying pahak, pahak, Lolo said: "They're calling for you,"
and everyone laughed. He never held them, but he let

them take twenty-five instead of ten centavos from the cash
register for school lunch money, and when they'd hear

ducks making their noises, they'd always think of Lolo,
even after they'd flown away to different continents,

even after the cats had been long dead, and new cats
began to eat the scraps he brought back from lunch.

WITH

❡

1.

The twins

Drink their mother

Through a rope

The words become

Bed after bed

Of daffodils gone wet

The night divides

Over and over

Emptied into a glass

Figurines of St. Francis buried

Beneath the house in little coffins

And when the world yawns

2.

The twins love their aunts and uncles,

While brothers

Grow out from houses with ironing boards,

The electric fan

Buzzes with the flies

It is always morning, the rooster speaks
Solitary

They find themselves imagining angels
As if they could be

Swept in and out with a broom

The Angels are when
And much more carefully where

Sunlight
Car light

Open windows
The dried fish
Take the air

Love smells like drowning but isn't mother

Discovering us
Beneath the floorboards

3.
The twins want to be alone
But are always with,

To each other,
They are a smell

That cannot be

Removed by washing
Or leaving—

To be singled out,
To be disappeared

Still their hands had a twin
Their eyes, a double

Quadrupled

After death, does one feel
The image

Of the self, repeating
Over and over

4.
In their sleep,
They dream of mother

In multiple
Her breasts always

Repeating themselves
In having, halving

Her legs
Always

Boys and boys and boys
With candlewick lips

To be lit

WHICH CAME FIRST

1.

When I was six years old
in the Philippines, The One-Eyed
Chicken spoke to me.
It clucked my name: *Marianne.*
It batted its wings. It made me come
to its coop, demanding I riffle
my fingers through its plume.
It pecked at my knees. Chicken
came first. Blood came second.
The truth is and always has been:
The chicken is forgiven. It showed
me what I was full of. The answer
is machinery. The answer is a red,
tinny fluid. The answer is bone
and salt and water and trash,
tons and tons of human waste.

2.

The lie is and always has been
that I came first. We were seventeen

and in the back of his Jimmy.
My rural love, my four-wheeler sweetie,

he believed and still believes
that he had taught me how

to come. Quickly. And hard.
I crowed (yes, crowed!) rooster-style

to fool him. I flapped my arms
into wings. I exclaimed: "That was

amazing!" But the truth is
and has always been he had come

first and last. I made him
come both. Cracked him open,

showed him the oversized chicken
that lay inside. We are all egg, until

The One-Eyed Chicken speaks
our name. Until The One-Eyed Chicken

sits on our face, until it teaches us
how to do chicken things, how to fly

the chicken way, which is to say,
close to the earth.

3.

Which came first:

the coming or the desire

to come? The first time I came

I laughed so hard I nearly fell

onto the basement floor. My body

tingled as a million chicks

pecked from the inside, urging

to be made free. I hatched. The egg

did not come first without chicken.

Post-hatch, the chicken is

and will always be somewhat egg,

as the spirit is always somewhat body,

as doubt and faith are always

somewhat intertwined, as the second

coming always contains some

reference to the first.

4.

There is no egg,

no first or last, only Love.

Love, they say, if made to bleed,

would bleed infinite. Love, if made a bed,

would come infinite. Love,

if giving head, would swallow

the whole egg raw. Now as an adult, I set

The Chicken loose in a coop

in the backyard. It clucks so much

I no longer hear it. My children

ask their questions. "Why does the sun

come down, why do the worms come out

after rain?" I hold them close, I wipe

the shell off their faces. They ask:

"Which came first?" I tell them

The One-Eyed Chicken comes

when it is ready to come,

and only when it is not invited.

SEAFOOD CITY

I am eating milkfish in the desert, and for dessert,
some pandesal, and I aspire to be

low-carb, but pandesal reminds me of my mother's

      hands and I wish I were holding them now
in Michigan, singing "Love Will Keep Us Together"—

I'll be her Captain, she my Tennille. But alas the desert
and the dessert

      claim me. Soon I'll climb
into my Honda CR-V. I'll sing along to the golden

oldies and coast down Flamingo
      with the AC blasting.   Maybe later I'll

go to a Motown impersonation show where the same
person will play both Tina
and Diana. There are so many Filipinos

in Seafood City with Honda CR-Vs, like the one I drive.
      The other day,

in the parking lot, I unlocked

someone else's car, I nearly drove away until I discovered

the boxes of Spam in the back seat
      and the general lack of pandesal crumbs

on the floor. It was an easy mix-up. A rosary
also dangled from my car's rearview
      mirror, white beads,

gold chain. My dad hung it there just before he left me
alone in a city

with nearby brothels and machine-gun-and-burger
joints, penny slots
in grocery stores, my roulette addiction

at its peak. In July, when the desert sun is raging

and unkind, the rosary will melt off,

and I won't even notice.

The truth is I don't deserve my desert dessert, the sweet
hot sun, this meat bun, this pandesal

      on the tongue.
How does one live forever in Paradise, what
does it mean to feel

      deserted, to feel desperate

for something sacred, for some substance
to soothe the soul? The Motown cover band

is garbage, but I'll dance anyway. It will remind me
of the real thing,

and by real thing, I mean, my mother on the microphone

with no makeup, flour
beneath her nails, the dough kneaded, all of us needing

to hear her sing "My Girl" or "Please Mr. Postman"

and Dad at the Adoration Chapel kneeling before
the pandesal of Christ, praying for our souls.

THE LIVES OF SAINTS

My father emails me a quote by St. Thérèse of Lisieux, but I
learn that Thérèse

would not have liked the largeness of the email. It is too big
for the little flower, the saint

                of little things. I learn from Wikipedia
that Thérèse wished to remain small—or little enough to be
lifted

into Heaven—and that she "had dreamed of the desert to
which God would someday lead her."

The Internet is an afterlife, and if it is a desert, it is
the American Mojave, where one might find

                      desolate plains of red
dirt, and also pockets of neon and billboards and clubs

where a towheaded DJ presses his headphone against his ear
making a room

bubble like a shoal of bream. I'm not sorry about this desert to
which God somehow led sweet, little Thérèse of Lisieux.

Perhaps the Internet is not the desert she would've chosen but
I am happy

for her, nonetheless. She shares her space with videos of otters
holding hands, with Instagram models,

                              who, like saints, are
idols with bios and backstories, their pictures like the images
on holy cards.

These thoughts, however, are not what my father hoped

I'd take away from his email which said: "Miss no opportunity
to make some small sacrifice." My father, the Catholic,

worries about my soul, and this worry appears to me as a vision
in the form of an email

in my inbox, a quote from St. Thérèse, the little saint
of littleness.

Perhaps, he should be worried.

I pray to no saint, and my little sacrifice for the day is to go
to work and to refrain

                        from picking at the dry patch of skin on
the back of my scalp and to smile and smile and smile until
5 p.m.

when my hot car will melt away that charitable cheese
from my face, when I'll wish

for some miracle to swoop me up and out and far from Florida
and into a pile of fresh sky-grated snow.

                        I am not sad, no.
My emotional state is hush-colored; that yellow-green shush
of cicadas makes me nothing again,

when all I want is to be something. A few years ago, my parents
set me down in front of a DVD

about a flashy Filipina visionary named Emma who claimed to
see apparitions

              of the Virgin Mary and who picked gemstones
from her forehead and whose body

sweated golden glitter when she saw her visions, and I realized then
the high demand for sainthood,

how badly everyone around her needed that sparkling
presence—how much they wanted the thorns

that gathered on her forehead, like sunburn or spectators
around an accident. We all think: here is the evidence

to confirm that we are not, in fact, nothing,

that we are the chosen animals. There is no irony to the fact
that the abbreviation for saint

is the same as the one for street. Saints are the ground

on which we walk. And without them, we are merely falling or
floating or treading, or we are simply here,

standing with ourselves in our rooms, in our little world. I
check my phone for notifications, but everything

is quiet as an empty bathtub. I check the sky for a sky and find
no sign,

feel only the skyness one feels during
twilight. God knows I am a cavern that refuses to be filled.

FORGIVE THEM FOR THEY DO NOT KNOW WHAT

Today: I can't stop watching the video
        of the Pope yelling at the man

in the crowd. The Pope is pulled forward
        so hard he nearly falls onto another

enthusiastic fan in a chair. He is pissed!
        Yesterday: nada, boredom,

routine snow on already salted
        streets, but today: a man assaulted

the Pope by accident! Call the police!
        The Pope is yelling! A spectacle!

A drama! O, peaceful papa. O, holy father.
        "He's only human," the commenters

remark on social media, on which all things
        are called by their real name. Human.

I went to Mass this weekend with my folks.
        I hadn't been for months.

Above the altar hung a modern statue
        of Christ (who, I must say,

resembled the artist formerly known as Prince).
　　　　His body sparkled, he held

a wishbone, or was it the holy spirit? Bird
　　　　or bone? Who can tell the difference?

The priest looked like William H. Macy
　　　　and spoke of moral logic and intuition.

Afterward, we had brunch, ate eggs, smoked salmon,
　　　　ham sandwich. My intuition

said yes. Then my moral logic spoke to me.
　　　　Poor animals, it said, who died for my sins,

for my desire, my hunger, my anger. My mother
　　　　took photos of our plates with her

phone. On social media, crowds of people
　　　　applauded our croque-madame.

Again, the Pope yells at a man, a stranger
　　　　in Mexico, on my tenth

watch of the video, I see a flame in Pope's
　　　　eyes, a sort of passion, and I do,

now, wonder if the Pope has ever
　　　　had sex, and what he would be like,

though he probably never has, probably
  never will. His will is too great. But only

human. Call the police! Someone wanted
  a piece of the Pope, and now he's pissed.

Another person commented: "Forgive them
  for they do not know what," and it ended

there. None of them know what. But it's fine.
  I don't know what. You don't know what.

Pope don't know what. Wishbone-spirit knows.
  But he isn't human, not one bit.

· III.

DECEMBER 1998

You are dreaming of a brown Christmas
with people who have never trusted

snow. Christmas begins on the guitar,
and ends on the windowsill

where your uncles
in your father's hand-me-down T-shirts

lean on their elbows until early morning.
Here, the windows have no glass,

protect no secrets. This year, you ask
Santa Claus for an alarm clock

to keep you awake because you don't
want to shut your eyes

to the stringed lights on the banana leaves,
the paper lanterns dangling from houses,

Fall on your knees, oh hear—
Perhaps Santa is your drunken uncle

imparting wisdom, beating his neighbors
at chess, eating miniature green bananas,

lounging on reclining lawn furniture
with his open shirt, in his wide open

living room, yelling for his children—who
are older than you but smaller—to come

inside and eat. Or, Santa is your
mother who arrived on the islands

from a German America in the middle
of the night holding her groggy children

(you) in her arms, making an entrance
with luggage filled with canned goods

and underwear. To the balikbayan,
loneliness is given in return. A desire to leave

after remembering the melancholic taste
of ripe lansones on the lips, how

your grandfather died before he met snow,
and how your grandmother lost

her legs to disease. *Fall on your knees, oh hear*
the heart quiver on the stringed instruments.

Still her ghost lingers, her legs reattached
by death. On these islands, white Christmas

is a play on words. Santa exists in theory.
But the dead exist in practice.

On the dining table, leave mangos for the dead,
rice, a plate of chocolate. Then, when all

is quiet, listen for footsteps on the roof
of their house, and do not shut your eyes.

VIEWING SERVICE

for Fabian Nudalo

From the Philippines, my cousin FaceTimes me, shows me

the coffin in Tito's bedroom. I stare at my phone
trying to say anything, but nothing follows. All I can think of

is that I don't remember the Bisaya word for head,
         for body. After a minute, the FaceTime video moves
into the dining room. My parents

appear on the screen and grin, as if ready for a selfie—"Hi, Yan,"
they greet me from oceans away. My mother's eyes
         carry sacks beneath them, souvenirs from jet lag

and weeping. Flies hover behind them over a plate
of sliced mangos.

And I think: What is the Bisaya word for fly, for fly home
         now? I notice my parents are glancing
at the corner of the screen, where a small box contains

         their image. Dad runs fingers
through his hair. Mom straightens her blouse. They were
once children on this island, nibbling

on banana-leaf rice, their shoulders rubbing
against other shoulders on the jeepney. Now, they only fly

home for the funerals. I take a screenshot of them. I try

to remember the Bisaya word for remember. After we hang up,
I type up a message in English. I won't press Send. I will
think about Tito. His rice-white teeth, his hairless arms.

How he told me stories about ogres and white ladies,

how, on the microphone, he'd sing: "talk in everlasting
words and dedicate them all to me,"

how, at the airport the last time I saw him, he walked

slowly, bone-heavy, burdensome as a church.

SOME WORDS OF THE AFORESAID
HEATHEN PEOPLES

In *Magellan's Voyage: A Narrative Account of the First Circumnavigation*, Antonio Pigafetta includes a list of Bisaya words and their translations called "Some Words of the Aforesaid Heathen Peoples," words he learned on the island of Cebu.

In this list, he translates the Bisaya word for "mother-of-pearl," but not the Bisaya word for "mother."

I wonder if his readers—Europeans—found this strange, the exclusion. Perhaps they thought: These heathen peoples did not have a word

for "mother." These heathens did not have mothers at all, only mothers-of-pearl. They were born, not from women,

but from milky shells that tumbled onto shore. Or, maybe, these heathen peoples were never born, only written into life. If a tree falls in the forest with no European to hear it, did it really exist before the 1500s? Did it have a mother to speak of? Was her name Pigafetta?

*

My mother's name is Patricia.
My mother's mother was Guadalupe
Mabano, an illiterate entrepreneur,
who made her living selling ripe fruit

at the market. She was obsessed
with food, afraid of starvation.
When she arrived home after my mother
had fallen asleep, she fed her

without waking her, shoving spoon
after spoon of rice and kamungay
leaves into her mouth. I imagine
she feared my mother would

dream hungry. My mother chewed
without tasting, took a full supper
before she woke up, surprised
at the grains of rice that lingered in her

throat, the fullness of her belly
beneath her shirt. Years later, in the States,
my mother, a diabetic, saw a new doctor
who doubled her prescription of insulin.

My father pressed the needle into her
stomach before bed, and that night she

dreamed she was a child screaming:
"I'm so hungry, Mama, so hungry,"

and she awoke out of the dream
into an America where her blood sugar
was down to 60, where her mother
had been dead for years.

*

Most likely, Pigafetta's list of heathen words excluded the word for "mother" because the items he named were limited to merchandise, that is, objects or elements that could be exported

Mana	Cinnamon
Boloto	Boats
Pilla	Silver
Tipai	Mothers-of-pearl

Why then did he include

Camat	Hand
Illoc	Armpits
Boto	Genitals
Dila	Tongue

Pigafetta sold my mother's tongue in the form of his book all over Europe. He said the language was more valuable than cloves.

My mother still speaks to me in this language, now influenced by Spanish words, and I can understand, but can't speak it. These are words I forget until I hear them.

*

My mother can't wait until I am
a mother. She wishes to be a lola,
a grandmother. But I don't want
to get pregnant. I want to learn
and relearn this language,
our history, again and again.
Maybe I lack courage. Maybe I fear
the uncertainty of the future,
so I hold the past with both arms.
Or perhaps, because my husband
is a White American, I worry
my child won't need to learn
her past. I worry my daughter will
enter the world with three navels,
and will never know the various bodies
that came together to feed her.
Word for "navel" in Bisaya is "pusod."
Pigafetta includes this in his list
of heathen words. He does not
include the word for "forgetting."

*

When I ask my mother questions about her childhood, her answers tumble onto shore. She becomes the debris of a broken ship. She overflows, overflowers. Discovers

new feelings she can't express eloquently in English. Discovers herself—all of her—

again in the retelling. She awakens with leaves in her throat, Bisaya in her teeth, a belly full of her mother tongue.

When I think about my lola, my mother, myself—I recognize all the things that have been and will be forgotten, so I'm writing this down,

like Pigafetta, alongside his list of words, all of them ours, all of them heathen.

IN DEFENSE OF KARAOKE

But the microphone was always a cradle / Elvis and Patsy Cline /
Sinatra Nat King Cole / Sharon Cuneta / Lea Salonga

my god / your grandfather's throat was the moon / and when
at the meat market / the man shaves a pig's face

and croons / I just want your extra time / and your / Kiss / along
with the television behind him / the body reverberates / the body

echoes aches / the lungs are your mother's kitchen / where she
sings Usahay / oh sigh / lyrics unspool past your school / past

the vast pool of motorbikes / Jeepneys / past the oranges past
the barefootedness / into your husband into your son / into

America / atop Lake Michigan /around which you drive
in your car and trees / scroll past fast akin to the lyrics of your

song / because you always / sing I'm so excited and I just / can't
hide it / because you always are / and you always can't

you always will / will yourself to life when you have no choice /
or voice / unravel into the microphone and listen / to yourself

double / miss your mother father brother / kiss their photographs /
kiss America / learn to love it / until you learn the lyrics by heart.

CEBU CITY

1.

The beetle swings
on a string

held by children. Their mothers

laugh at their fear.
The children are put to bed early

and the mothers wake
at dawn to cook, they feed

their daughters first,
then their sons.

Today we awaken to the lighting
of stoves. This is a community

of kitchens;
suns and cousins,

downpours.

My cousin C. and I hike up
the muddy hill during a rain,

a man sleeps in the corn,

I walk speedily past,
in need of exercise, I feel

my body heavy.

This is how I worry:
my body, my body—

C. says I am preoccupied,
that I am homesick

and tired of her.

We reach the top
where Cebu City
is new and one color
behind the fog.

2.
C. hangs our wet clothing
outside and takes them down
before dusk. She is afraid

the ghosts nearby will wear
our shirts and shoes.
A man in his home

just the other day
collapsed
and died, his body

is behind his house in a box
beneath the grotto.

His ghost knocks
on neighbor windows
during rainfall.
His ghost wears our raincoats,

raising discarded
newspapers over his head,
a posed, human gesture.

We keep mangos
outside our door
for him to eat.

C. is subservient.

She cleans my room
though I ask her to stop.
She sweeps out the dust.

When my
parents die,
what will I
owe her?

When she dies,
what will she take
of mine to wear?

She is my cousin,
one of many cousins.

My body, I fret. My body.

3.
We speak
to each other in multiple,

her words are seeds
and seeds and seeds.

Inside me, I can't find
the materials that make this
language, and yet

Bisaya

digs a part of me
out of the ground.

Bisaya turns the mud
of her and grows
out of her after rain

and what becomes
is something

stony, allegiant;
holy and with—

Now, my cousin calls
me long-distance
and we have nothing

to say. She was once
asked to come with us,
but she chose to stay.

SOMETHING BORROWED

The names of orbits, the names
       of Uncles, the names of plants

all memorized or gathered or buried
       with the seeds. I have never grown

weary of reading the labels of spices,
       ingredients of a potion, desert trees.

Never grown tired of counting
       the seconds between lightning

and its boom, the gongs of the big clock
       as it adds the hours that have

passed since midnight, when the college
       is still asleep, and the students are

forgetting the answers to their teacher's
       great questions. As we forget

the names of orbits, planets. The day
       they married. The day he died.

That day was Monday. August,
       and it was hot outside.

COUNTERARGUMENT THAT GOES ALL THE WAY AROUND

Antonio Pigafetta, is the world reversible? I'm not good at math, but if
    I could run
backwards, I would travel eastward. I already spend my days
    regressing,
crashing into fragile ornaments, in search of what I've left behind.
Digging a hole to China, I remember I don't have to do this;

everyone knows they can explore their origins without
fighting off blind cave fish, elusive nematode worms,
giant orb-weaving spiders, the earth's molten core. What if we
head out on a voyage instead? We'll sail all the way around.

If we make it without dying, then we can celebrate over
jugs of palm wine, as we move against the current, against the present,
    on this
king-unsanctioned circumnavigation, or perhaps *retro-navigation*, of
    the heart.
Listen to the heart's sea, all the creatures hiding there. What is their

manner of living? Do they go naked, are their faces painted white? "I'll
    tell you
now," interrupts my mother, as we dock at the Island of Hands.
"On a sheet of waterleaf paper, your Lola learned to write my name.
Patricia is a word she knew how to spell. She was a musician.
    Her voice

quivered as she sang with a guitar, plucking round, sour notes,
round as a belly, round as a world that spins." Suddenly, our ship
     drifts away,
south toward the Island of Moving Feet. There, my dad says,
     "Lolo came
to the Philippines from China for friendship, safety,

untethered growth. He was never good at math. He always wanted
very much to go back to China, to get on the boat and row back-
wards, toward the setting sun, but he couldn't find home on the
XY coordinate plane. So, he stayed.

Young, strong, he grew his business, remained on the island of
Zzubu forever, making country out of family, family out of country."
Zipping through this island are giants. The giants are weeping.
You've seen giants before, Tony, but why are they crying? You're my

xenagogue, Tony, please impart your wisdom as we move
westward, past the Cape of Forgotten Obstacles, through the Strait of
Violent Returns. Here the trees are sinking into the soil. Here,
underwater, there is no place to anchor, no story to tell.

This is a desert of no cacti, tundra of no winter birds. Suddenly,
     Lola appears.
She says: "The body is infinite. It goes all the way around. It grows
round in the belly, round as a world. I created bodies. Ten, all men,
quite tall. Giants in my belly. But I wanted to leave,

perhaps the heart is the best navigator, the captain-general
of the living. I do not wish to go backwards. I want the future, where
nobody can see me, where I can be alone with myself, my M&Ms,
my America, my years, increasing with each drag of the
          Capri cigarette."

Lonely on the Bay of Tired Virgins, I take Lola's hand, and she
knows the direction. Adrift on the water, she makes us strawberry
Jell-O. If I lift it up to my face, I see the world is in fact as rosy as
I want it to be, as rosy as you saw it, Tony. Suddenly, my
          great-great Lolo

hatches from an egg sitting on an iceberg in the middle of the water.
"Go and bring him to us," my Lola says, "and listen to what he has
          to say."
For a moment, I am worried, as he is naked from the waist down. He
enters our ship, and says: "I have never been good at math, but I

do understand the way patterns blossom. It all adds up!
Coordinates tell you where you stand. The past hammers
behind the present, and at the very edge of it all, we see through the
          Jell-O.
Around the world, we are the same people. We have merely moved
          our feet."

ACKNOWLEDGMENTS

I am grateful to the editors of the following journals, in which versions of these poems appear:

BOAAT, "On Buzz Aldrin's Birthday," "Origin Story"

Denver Quarterly, "With"

Hobart, "Jet Lag"

The Journal, "When We Lived in Germany"

The Margins, "Lansing Sinulog Rehearsal, 2010," "My Mother Tells Me about Lolo"

Michigan Quarterly Review, "Love Song for Antonio Pigafetta," "Some Words of the Aforesaid Heathen Peoples"

Mississippi Review, "The Lives of Saints"

Poetry Northwest, "In Defense of Karaoke"

Quiddity, "Cebu City," "Which Came First"

The Rumpus, "When the Man at the Party Said He Wanted to Own a Filipino"

Shenandoah, "Forgive Them for They Do Not Know What," "Momotaro in the Philippines"

SLICE, "A Country of Beautiful Women"

Tampa Review, "Viewing Service"

West Branch, "December 1998"

Witness, "Something Borrowed"

In 2017, the poem "Origin Story" appeared in *The Orison Anthology, Vol. 2* (edited by Luke Hankins, Nathan Poole, and Karen Tucker). In 2019, "When the Man at the Party Said He Wanted to Own a Filipino" appeared in *Ink Knows No Borders: Poems of the Immigrant and Refugee Experience*, an anthology from Seven Stories Press (edited by Patrice Vecchione and Alyssa Raymond). In 2020, "December 1998" and "Origin Story" appeared in *The World I Leave You: Asian American Poets on Faith and Spirit*, published by Orison Books (edited by Leah Silvieus and Lee Herrick).

I am very grateful to my poetry teachers who mentored and supported me in my writing throughout the years: Diane Wakoski, Claudia Keelan, Donald Revell, and James Kimbrell.

To Sarah Gorham, Jeffrey Skinner, and the amazing Sarabande Books team: I cannot thank you enough. It has been a joy and an honor to work with you.

Abiding thanks to my friends, many more than can be named here. I'm especially grateful to the following individuals for their help in shaping some of these poems: Kaitlyn Andrews-Rice, Michael Berger, Eleanor Boudreau, Geoff Bouvier, Maile Chapman, Olivia Clare, Austin Ely, William Fargason, Katie Flynn, Tanya Grae, Barbara Hamby, Jean Ho, Jessie King, Kien Lam, Maureen Langloss, Paige Lewis, Joleen Long, Brandi Nicole Martin, Dorsey Olbrich, Lee Patterson, Dustin Pearson, Rosemary Powers, Becky Robison, Amy Rossi, Denise Weber, Josh Wild, and Richard Wiley.

Special thanks to Clancy for his brilliant feedback, delicious cooking, and enduring love. These poems would not exist without you.

Deepest gratitude to my family in the Philippines, the US, and Canada. This book is for you.

MARIANNE CHAN grew up in Stuttgart, Germany, and Lansing, Michigan. She holds degrees from Michigan State University and the University of Nevada, Las Vegas. Her poems have appeared in *Michigan Quarterly Review*, *Cincinnati Review*, *Ninth Letter*, *West Branch*, *The Rumpus*, and elsewhere. Currently, she is pursuing a PhD in Creative Writing and Literature at the University of Cincinnati, where she is a Yates Fellow.

SARABANDE BOOKS is a nonprofit literary press located in Louisville, KY. Founded in 1994 to champion poetry, short fiction, and essay, we are committed to creating lasting editions that honor exceptional writing. For more information, please visit sarabandebooks.org.